Understanding
Colonial
Handwriting

UNDERSTANDING COLONIAL HANDWRITING

Harriet Stryker-Rodda

Baltimore
GENEALOGICAL PUBLISHING CO., INC.

Originally published in
New Jersey History (Spring-Summer 1980)
This revised edition published by
Genealogical Publishing Co.,Inc.
Baltimore, 1986, 1987, 1989, 1993
Copyright © 1986 by
Harriet Stryker-Rodda
All Rights Reserved
Library of Congress Catalogue Card Number 85-82529
International Standard Book Number 0-8063-1153-3
Made in the United States of America

Understanding Colonial Handwriting

It is no longer necessary, as it once was, for genealogists and family historians to use a multitude of original documents for research. Since the middle of this century genealogical and historical primary source materials have been widely transcribed, translated, typed, xeroxed, microfilmed, microfiched, photo-offset, printed and reprinted. Some of the work done is excellent. Some is execrable.

With the computerization of genealogical data, however, glaring errors have crept into source materials that should drive the careful researcher back to the originals. If microfiche or microfilm of the originals are available, the researcher may find the same problems in reading that the computer programmer finds. Knowing how to read material other than the printed word, therefore, remains an essential aspect of all effective genealogical and historical research.

Recourse to original records, in whatever form, assures the researcher that no one has tampered with the content or the physical construction of the record. The changing styles of letter formation and the condition of the paper may present problems to the uninitiated. To analyze such a document we must understand its history, its purpose, its tools, even its scribe and his manner of writing.

We tend to forget that handwritten documentation, now so highly prized and used by genealogists, was not prepared for them. Each document had its own specific purpose. *Diaries* were kept by individuals who had a special, personal incentive. *Letters* were a means of communication. *Wills* were prepared to provide for descendants through disposal of property. *Deeds* were written to provide legal title to a carefully specified area and recorded to make the deal binding on all participating parties. *Church Records* were kept for ecclesiastical reporting to the church authorities or, in some instances, as surrogate records for local government. None of these, or any similar genealogically-useful source material, was prepared for the present-day researcher in family history.

When such documentation has survived the ravages of historical events it is truly a miracle—a miracle that in the 20th century there is so much remaining that carries special messages from the penman to the present reader. Among the messages to be read, there is also a revelation of the scribe and his tools, the real or implied history of people in time and place. All this is in a colonial document, awaiting interpretation.

The American colonial period began in the 17th century and extended through most of the 18th century. Any handwriting done in those two centuries was deeply influenced by the standards of writing in Europe, where writing was considered an *Art.* Until the middle of the 16th century in Europe the ability to write was considered beneath a gentleman's dignity. Writing was left entirely to scribes, secretaries, or cloistered priests who studied to perfect themselves in the *art* which then closely followed precise, hand-printed forms.

When permanent settlements in the American colonies were founded, it was against the background of a Europe fighting the last of its religious wars, the Thirty Years War (1618-1648). When it ended, the Holy Roman Empire was fragmented, Germany and her militant princes powerless. The modern state system of Europe was emerging. France and French ways and styles would dominate the European continent until the defeat of Napoleon in 1815 at Waterloo. Italian modes were beginning to be recognized. England was becoming a world power.

As the printing press in the mid-15th century gradually displaced the scribe and the illuminator of manuscripts, these skilled people found it necessary to change their occupations. Some became writing masters. Some found employment in expanding government offices where good handwriting was a requisite. Penmanship came out of the monastery and attracted people as a means of livelihood. A natural result of this was the development of copybooks for instruction. From 1600 there was a continuous stream of copybooks published in Europe. They were small and were illustrated with woodcuts showing the author's own style of writing. There were as many styles of handwriting as there were authors. Each had his own style, held his pen in his own way and taught handwriting in the bounds of his own geographical area. Some became traveling teachers and moved freely from place to place. The first English copybook was one prepared by two Frenchmen, Jehan de Beauchesne and John Baildon, called *A Book Containing Diverse Sortes of Hands,* published in London in 1571. It emphasized the Italian style of handwriting which had become important earlier in the 16th century as a result of its beauty and clarity.

Before 1650 Latin was the official court and ecclesiastical language throughout Europe. All official documents were written in Latin. Time was important then, as now, so most of the writing styles were based on abbreviations of Latin words and phrases which allowed an economy of pen motions. Thus there grew up among scribes many individual forms of shorthand. The handwriting became so highly personal and stylized that one man's writing was nearly unrecognizable by any but his own students. Eventually, it became necessary to systematize and standardize the forms of the various abbreviations of Latin phrases within each individual language's area of influence, and in diplomatic interchange.

One of the highly revolutionary ideas of the Commonwealth in 1649 in England was that English should become the official language for all domestic administrative purposes. It was ordered that records of all kinds were to be written "in an ordinary, usual and legible hand and character." That law was effective for only a short time. With the restoration of Charles II to the throne of England, Latin and the stylized "Court Hands" were back in their full glory. It wasn't until 1713 that English law again provided that scribes and clerks once more resort to common English and legible handwriting. In the interim the American colonies were developing.

Even a law as demanding as this one could not immediately erase the writing habits and speed devices that had developed among scribes and teachers of writing. A change of this magnitude takes time. It needed a new generation, but their teachers would be the older scribes who were persistent in their continued use of Latin abbreviations, their own word forms and phonetic spellings. Despite the numbers of copybooks available for teaching, some odd combinations of script, abbreviations and spelling lasted a long time. Some very old short forms persisted in the English colonies and are used even today: the ampersand sign for the word *and* (&); the sign for the word *at* (@); the abbreviation of the Latin *et cetera* to *etc.*

Of course all the scribes in the American colonies were not English. They were Dutch, French, German, Jewish, Spanish, Swedish, and of many other nationalities. Each man brought his own language when he immigrated, and it was inevitable that colonial documents would reflect national backgrounds. One of the difficulties in translating Dutch colonial documents in the State of New York, for instance, is that a scribe trained by a French or Belgian handwriting teacher had difficulty recording rapidly in the Dutch language. When the British took over the colony in the late 17th century, another change occurred among the Dutch scribes who continued in government offices. They had to change to writing exclusively in English. As a consequence some men in high places in the old government in New Netherland withdrew from office because their speaking and writing knowledge of English was so imperfect.

By 1640 the first forest-clearing and land-settling had been accomplished in the American colonies. A second and, in some colonies, a third generation had been born. The need for educating these children became urgent. Some churches had established schools in a few colonies, and *Symm's Free School* in Virginia and *Boston's Latin School* in Massachusetts had just been established, but the teachers were mostly European born and trained. Moreover, these few schools could not reach out to educate all of the children. In the thirteen colonies it has been estimated there were about 52,000 persons at this time, few of whom knew how to write much more than their names. In general, if education was extended to children in their settlements or villages, at home or in inadequate schools, reading, writing and ciphering were all it was believed most of them would ever need. In the Dame Schools children were taught writing and ciphering through the use of a copybook. Very often that copybook was a series of pages sewn together by the teacher. Sentence models and letters were often just drawn on a child's slate by the teacher and the child copied them below.

Today recording is so highly mechanized that handwriting is reduced to a minor place in the school curriculum. An appreciation of early handwriting is obtained only through an understanding of its history and practices, but we should also consider its tools.

First, let us consider the pen. There were no graphite pencils. Graphite had not yet been encased in sweet-smelling cedar whittling wood. Pens bore no resemblance to our current ballpoints with their self-contained ink. Pens were simple tools made from feathers. Quill pens were first introduced in the Middle Ages. Goose feathers were most popular, but swans, hens and turkeys contributed their share. The good feathers that were to be used for the best pens were plucked from live birds. Excrescences were removed and the quill was heated or soaked in hot water before shaping with a penknife. In the early schools a very important part of the work of the teacher was sharpening quill pens for the day's use by the students.

The penknife, so essential to a proper shaping of the quill, was necessarily a sharp little instrument and much prized by its owner. In August 1776, when General Howe was encamped on Staten Island, there was recorded in his Orderly Book an indication of the high value placed upon such a tool: "Lost, a small green handled Penknife with Two Blades in a Case whoever brings it to Head Quarters will receive Two Dollars reward."

Before the invention of printing, the quill was cut with a chisel-shaped edge. This produced a variation in the width of the stroke depending on the direction in which the pen was moved. Various chisel shapes were developed. They produced a variation in widths and in the amount of pressure that could be applied without breaking the quill. The so-called *chancery writing* was done with this kind of pen, with its edge held at a constant 45° angle to the paper. It made a thin stroke as the pen moved up, and a thick stroke if it moved down, giving the full width of the nib. If it was moved in a curve, the result was a shading. Left-handed persons gave the paper a left cant and used a pen with a left-skewed chisel cut; right-handed persons did just the opposite. Good writing results were determined by the cut of the pen, the way it was held, the position of the paper, the slant of the pen's edge and its flexibility.

No one knows now who was responsible, or when the great discovery was made that gradually changed handwriting. It was found that a small hole in the nib would permit a longer writing span from one dip into the inkpot, because the hole would act as a minute reservoir. This increased the writers' speed, but it also created the running together of words. Even so, handwriting remained very time-consuming until the beginning of the 17th century.

Not too long before the first settlers arrived in America, there were two important developments in the art of writing. One was a change in the quill pen from the square chisel cut to a pointed cut that gave the pen greater flexibility. This change was reflected in early American handwriting. With the pointed quill the letters could still be formed with contrasting light and dark lines by exerting pressure. It was discovered that this more flexible tool made it possible to connect letters more clearly, to save time and energy, and that better separation of words offered greater clarity. It also increased speed.

There were some disadvantages. The pointed quill made it easier to jab the pen into the paper, creating inkspots that could not be removed. It has been said by calligraphers that the pointed pen is largely responsible for the sorry state of handwriting today because common writing lost its precision and artistic features.

The second development grew out of the first. With the old style chisel-edge pen, letters had been made large, all the same

The pointed quill pen
remained in use until
the 1830s.

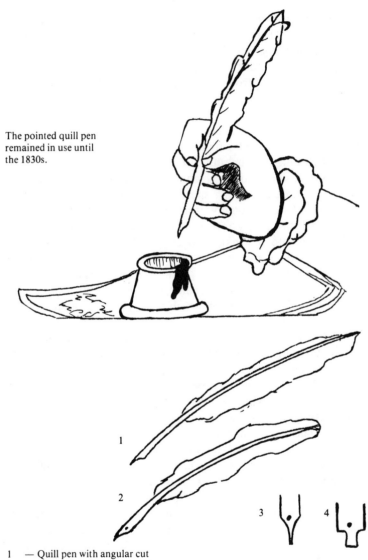

1 — Quill pen with angular cut
2 — Quill pen with ink well added
3 — Front view of nib
4 — Stub cut of nib with well

size, filling a two-line space. With the advent of the pointed cut, the pen could be held at any comfortable angle. Now, small letters corresponding in size to the printing machines' lower case, could be made between four imaginary lines instead of two, and the writing could be controlled so that the tops of tall letters such as small *b, d, l, k,* the old *s,* and *t* could be evenly swung to uniform heights.

The pointed quill remained in common use in the colonies and states until 1830 when the modern steel pen nib was introduced. It was not flexible like the quill. Because of its rigidity, there were limitations to the shading which it could produce. The steel nib, however, increased writing speed and produced more rhythmic and flowing letters as handwriting moved ever further away from 17th- and 18th-century forms. With the steel nib there was less need to dip into the inkpot so frequently. It also sparked the search for non-corrosive inks and the invention of innovative kinds of metal points and pens. The federal census records taken in 1790, 1800, 1810, 1820 and some in 1830 were taken with quill pens dipped into an inkpot which went along with the census taker.

The ink into which the quill was dipped was quite different from modern ink. Early inks were made from oak apples or galls, those swellings on trees caused by the parasitic gall fly. Copper sulfate, then called copperas or vitriol, and the sap or gum from trees, were mixed with the galls in large wooden tubs and stirred frequently for two or three weeks. The resulting thick, sticky, odorous mass was diluted with water and used as ink. Galls contain tannic acid, and if combined with iron salt, produce a purplish-black compound. When used for writing, this ink appeared as a dark purple that grew darker with age. We see it today on surviving documents as brown.

Some inks were made with lamp black, but unlike so-called iron ink, they did not combine with the paper, but tended to crack or wear off. Iron ink bites into the surface of the paper and becomes a part of it. An ink-filled quill pen jabbed into the surface of a sheet of paper, in time, produced first a spreading stain, then a hole. As the stain dried it became more and more brittle and broke away, leaving only the outline of a letter. There is evidence on the periphery of the way the ink stained the paper. In photocopies of original documents these ink stains will appear as shadows that may partially obscure portions of other letters.

The third tool of the scribe was his paper. When we consult a colonial document we see a miracle of survival. Intent upon grasping its message, we often fail to realize that it has survived the vicissitudes of war, vermin, weather and human neglect. Its own inherent ills are foxing, brown spot, splits along the folds, and fading. It certainly is not in the pristine state it was when it was written.

If a document was written before 1750 in this country you may be sure the paper was an immigrant. Paper-making in the colonies had its start late in the 17th century, but even after its feeble beginnings it was cheaper to import than to use domestic papers. All paper had a high rag content that gave it its lasting qualities. It did not contain self-destructing chemicals as do modern sulphide papers. It did contain some impurities, as evidenced by the foxing or spotting that exists in some of the documents which have survived.

In photocopies of documents, foxing, spotting, folds, wormholes and exposure to the elements will all be faithfully recorded. The researcher who uses them will not have to worry about leaving oil from his finger tips to make additional brown spots on the original which in time will further obscure content and message. Most modern researchers will prefer to study an old document from a copy which they can use in the peace and quiet of their own workroom, away from the inevitable distractions of the depository. As researchers, it is their duty to read as accurately as possible and interpret the message from another age.

It is at this point that inflexibility in reading habits must be laid aside. An efficient reader, for example, will find meaning in a group of symbols without needing to see each letter of which the whole is composed. Take yourself. You are about to read something which is neither typed nor printed, in a handwriting you have never seen before.

Before you start, know what the general subject of the

document will be. Is it a deed, a bail bond, a will? Every document has its own meaning, therefore its own language and purpose, its own context, which, when recognized and understood, will aid a reader who is not familiar with the handwriting.

You have found that there is a great deal of verbiage in many documents that seems to have been placed there just to annoy you. This is not the case. Those flowing phrases, replete with words having varying shades of meaning, were legally necessary in the situation and in the time and place. They were designed to prevent litigation. One clause of the contract might not have been sufficiently clarified with simpler, fewer words. Three centuries after England's original law calling for "usual and legible hand and character," we are still trying to move toward simplification of the legal language which was inherited from her. Don't let yourself be confused by the surviving legalese.

It is best to face the script bravely and just begin to read. Let your eyes move across the text, catching what they can, without attempting to read the individual letters or translate the words they form. At first reading, only a word or two may seem familiar. From these try to gather the meaning of the message. Continue the first rough reading to the end of the document. Do not stop along the way to figure out any of the individual problems. By this time the meaning should have appeared and the purpose of the document become evident. Then, make a second full reading. You may be surprised how quickly your own confidence will have grown. On the second try more words will have become familiar.

There is no set of rules that can be laid down for surmounting any of the difficulties you will still encounter on a third and fourth or fifth or sixth reading. You have to bring to bear your own imagination, your own ability to comprehend. The pressures of time and place, how you feel, how you control your impatience to get on with the job, all these can affect what one absorbs from reading anything. These same factors are equally important in reading unfamiliar manuscripts and documents.

Difficulties that arise during reading and re-reading may be due to the condition of the original paper or to the personal writing habits of the scribe. But they may also be due to the condition of the scribe's quill and ink. His personal abbreviations and word divisions or elisions, his spelling, his understanding of proper names and their spellings, can contribute to the reading difficulties. Perhaps the scribe's ignorance of the legal form has caused confusion. With no laws aimed at giving the public fully qualified lawyers, many of our early documents show the inadequacy of the system and the lack of preparation, or the low degree of legal skill, of the scribe.

Recognition of the scribe's style will come through persistent re-reading. His idiosyncracies will begin to take on a pattern and the recognized common words will start to make some sense. Holding a pencil in your hand and making an attempt on a piece of scrap paper to follow the scribe's manner of writing a letter or a word can be very helpful. Most helpful of all may be comparing letters and other words on the same page, noting similarities or variances. Your scribe may have used some of the earliest shorthand forms. Others may have found that the way to save time was to keep the pen on the paper, moving from word to word as rapidly as possible while the ink lasted on the pen. Some hung all their words together like beads on a string, as long as the ink held out. Punctuation as we know it today was not used, so don't look for it. In place of punctuation, sometimes, there were pauses indicated by dots. A dot on the line indicated a brief pause. A dot above a word indicated a full stop. A dot between words indicated phrase separation. Our present colon and a line through part of a name both meant an abbreviation of that name.

It is best to skip over difficult passages many times. Return to them once, perhaps, but it is better to leave them unresolved until all clear phrases and passages are extracted. Very often it will be found that the seemingly difficult phrase is not at all difficult. Familiarity with the material, the rapport established with the ghost of the scribe who made the record, and the determination to complete an accurate transcription will all combine to bring you success. Don't hesitate to lay the task aside for another day if it cannot be completed in one sitting. Some manuscripts take a long time to decipher.

If all this sounds time-consuming, it is. No hurried attempt at reading is going to force a document to give up all its treasures. Besides the actual deciphering of the writing, there must be interpretation. Any reading is an interpretive process. All those words in set phrases become just so many letters unless they set up a response in the reader based on *his* knowledge and *his* experience.

The searcher who finds an early document in French, German, Swedish or any other language unknown to him, is immediately faced with a problem. He may have studied a foreign language in school, but he probably is not equipped to read an early handwritten document in that language. Early manuscripts and records bear little relationship to the modern forms of their language. They contain, as does English, outmoded, colloquial words and phrases often difficult for the skilled translator, who must be able to read the script in addition to knowing the earlier forms of the language. The best advice for the family historian who must use such records is to seek the services of an expert.

Not all handwritten documents the American genealogist and historian will use will present reading difficulties. The official scribes, those clerks in government offices and lawyers' offices were not all poor penmen. They wrote as they had been taught to write, and much of the teaching had been good in the colonies. The handwriting of the man who was not well educated, more accustomed to pushing a plow than a pen, may present some problems. Diaries of uneducated men and women are not generally present-day source material because of their scarcity. Churchmen who kept records had fair hands, but we often wonder when we see the writing of their parishioners' names if their hearing and comprehension were adequate.

It may be necessary for the modern reader to become familiar with the letter forms used in various areas at particular times. Styles of letters brought from Europe became integrated here just as did the people who brought them - slowly. The forms the colonists brought persisted through our colonial period and did not change abruptly when we became a separate nation in the late 18th century. In fact, many of them continued to be used into the 20th century.

Letter Forms Found in American Handwriting 1640—1790

No firm date can be assigned to the transition from an old form to a single form of letters in colonial America. Some letters took longer to develop than did others. In the 150 years from 1640 to 1790 very clear script is found in some documents and as a result they are a delight to work with. It is equally true that in that period there were scribes whose handwriting cannot be fully deciphered. In this period which produced about five 30-year generations busy with wresting a living from soil and sea, a basic knowledge of writing, signing the name and reading, with some basic "figuring" were about all that was considered educationally necessary for males. In reading documents of this period, experience and imagination are of prime importance.

I and *J, i* and *j,* remained largely interchangeble into the beginning of the 19th century. The reverse tail loop of lower case *q* became standard as the *g* with its loop end and rounded top developed. Lower case *u* seems to have fared better than *v* as it developed. However, the *v* made with a diagonal upward stroke tended to disappear when combined with other letters.

Illustrations overleaf

*Confusion sometimes results in not correctly identifying *ϑ* as *e*, as in the following words:

ond = one   deep = deep   me = me

feel = feel   seal = seal

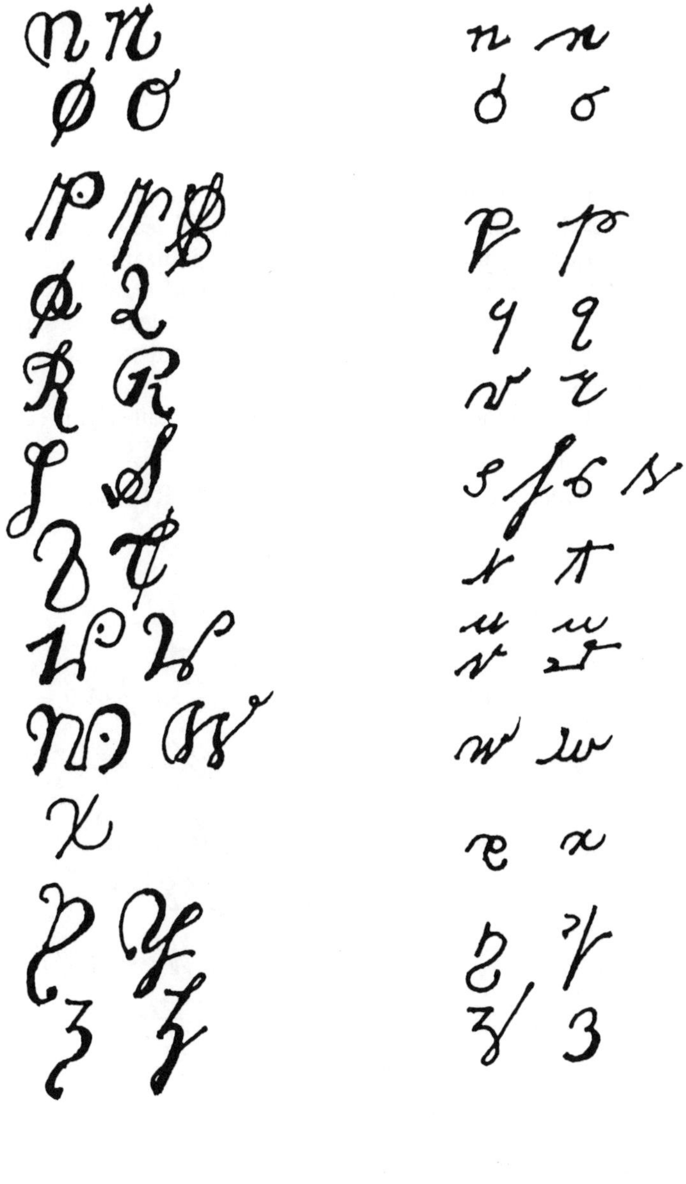

17th-Century Script
A Comparison

American colonial progress in the simplification of handwriting is very evident in the comparative chart below. Some letters still showed the influence of European writing masters. Some were still in development stage. Note the very simplified C in *C*harge. The lower case *g* and *s* were moving into capitalization as is seen in *G*ifts and *S*owwest *S*yde. *H, Q* and *W* had arrived as clear capitals. In *Turff and Twigg,* the small *g,* to at least one scribe, was no longer made like a lower case *y* closed at the top with a straight line.

Still in use was the mark over *u* that had originally signified the

ENGLISH			AMERICAN
$\mathcal{A}$	*a*	*All*	*All*
$\mathcal{B}$	*r*	*Brought*	*Brought*
tt	*c*	*Charge*	*Charge*
g	*ð*	*Devided*	*Devided*
$\mathcal{E}$	*ə*	*Easttate (estate)*	*Easttate*
ff	*ſ*	*Fulling Mill*	*Fulling Mill*
s	*g*	*Gifts*	*Gifts*
$\mathcal{E}$	*c*	*Heires*	*Heires*

difference between that letter and an *n* when rapidly written. Spelling had not yet been completely standardized. Note, for example, *Devided, Easttate, Heires, Priviledges.*

The common speech of the colonist who either dictated or wrote a deed is frequently found in such phrases as *Sowwest Syde.* *Turff and Twigg* is a lawyer's phrase, derived from English feudal law. It soon disappeared in the colonies, but William Penn used it in defense of his title to the Three Lower Counties in Delaware.

Capitals *I* and *J, U* and *V,* were still interchangeable, but lower case *u, v* and *w* were more clearly defined, as evident in Queen, Priviledges, Sowwest.

	said Isaac	*said Isaac*
I and J still interchangeable	Joseph	*Joseph*
	Know all Men	*Know all Men*
	Lawes	*Lawes*
	Negro	*Negro*
	Priviledges	*Priviledges*
	Queen	*Queen*
	Remainders	*Remainders*
	Sowwest Syde	*Sowwest Syde,*
	Turff and Twigg	*Turff and Twigg*
	Whereas	*Whereas*

English: from A. F. Bennett's *Guide for Genealogical Research* (1951)

American: from deeds and wills in various colonies

Name Forms and Signatures Found in Local Public Documents 1750—1820

Today given names in signatures continue to show individual styles of handwriting. This illustrated group of seven *Elizabeths* or their abbreviations, are clear and easily read, yet reveal the individual interpretation of letters from writing lessons. The first, second and fifth Elizabeths undoubtedly wrote Eliza, yet see how different each *E* and *z* is.

Mr. Elwood's name is used as an illustration here to show that not all names can be read with certainty. Was Mr. Elwood's first name Rion, Bion, Kron? This is the kind of signature which demands that the researcher have some previously collected information about the owner.

Signatures and names should be an important consideration for the researcher. It often becomes necessary to identify a person by the most commonly used form of his name or by a comparison of his signatures. This latter is not always easy. The three signatures of Caleb Bryant were offered as illustrations in a family history by a descendant who believed they were all written by the same man. Careful study of them shows basic differences and practically no similarities.

Ru*f*us Morse illustrates here the reason *s* and *f* need not be confusing: they were not written exactly the same by most scribes. Rufus Morse neatly used their differences in his careful signature. Ru*f*us Roe had another solution for the problem, while maintaining his very old-fashioned, early colonial capital *R*.

Finally, a very characteristic problem. The eight first names of these men show the continuing interchangeability of the *I* and the *J* which remained confusing for more than a generation into the 19th century.

Harriet Stryker-Rodda is a certified genealogist with over fifty years of experience as a researcher, teacher, lecturer and author. In her long and distinguished career she has enjoyed a great many honors. In 1981 she was made a Fellow of the New Jersey Historical Society "for scholarly contributions to history and genealogy," and in 1984 the New Jersey Historical Commission honored her "for outstanding service to public knowledge." She is perhaps best known as the author of *How to Climb Your Family Tree: Genealogy for Beginners.*

Her essay on colonial handwriting grew out of a lecture she has presented at least fifty times since 1969, beginning with the World Conference on Records in Salt Lake City. In 1980 the New Jersey Historical Society published a version of this lecture in its journal *New Jersey History,* which is the basis of this present work.

T|
GIFT

JIM WESTCOTT

SADDLEBACK
EDUCATIONAL PUBLISHING

red rhino
b**OO**ks®

Body Switch
The Cat Whisperer
Clan Castles
The Code
Fight School
Fish Boy
Flyer
The Garden Troll
Ghost Mountain
The Gift

The Hero of
  Crow's Crossing
Home Planet
I Am Underdog
Killer Flood
Little Miss Miss
The Lost House
The Love Mints
The Magic Stone
Out of Gas
Racer

Sky Watchers
The Soldier
Space Trip
Standing by Emma
Starstruck
Stolen Treasure
Too Many Dogs
World's Ugliest Dog
Zombies!
Zuze and the Star

With more titles on the way …

SADDLEBACK
EDUCATIONAL PUBLISHING
www.sdlback.com

ISBN-13: 978-1-62250-895-2
ISBN-10: 1-62250-895-5
eBook: 978-1-63078-027-2

Printed in Malaysia

21 20 19 18 17   4 5 6 7 8

1043865

Zeke

Age: 11

Favorite Breakfast: Froot Loops cereal with milk and sliced bananas

Secret Wish: wants his parents to be nice to each other

Favorite Hobby: rock hunting for gemstones

Best Quality: very open-minded

ANDREW

Age: would have been 11

Family Pet: a sheepdog named Rags (who can still see him)

Favorite Afterlife Stunt: going through walls and locked doors

Wanted to Be: a stand-up comedian

Best Quality: loves his family

1
TRAPPED

My mom and dad are opposites. They never agree.

OTHER OPPOSITES

"Zeke, let's go. Practice time. Let's do it. Three hundred kicks," Dad says.

"You don't have to. Soccer is supposed to be fun," Mom says.

"You baby him," Dad says. He says this a lot. "Come on."

"Well, Coach," she yells back. "Keep it up. He's gonna hate soccer. And you!"

I am trapped. I hate being in the middle.

"Tell your mom you like soccer," Dad yells.

"Tell your dad you hate it," Mom yells.

Still trapped.

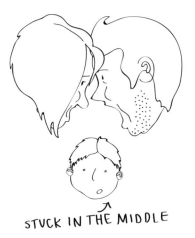

STUCK IN THE MIDDLE

They don't get it. Truth is, I like soccer a lot. I'm pretty good. But Dad is always in my face. Yelling at me in front of my team. He only yells at me.

I don't hate my dad. He just gets … excited.

Then Mom tells Dad something. Something I wish she hadn't. But I don't say anything. Wish I had. She says I want to quit the team. Because of him.

"This true, Zeke?" my dad asks in his coach's voice.

I look down. Can't say a word. He walks away.

Then he leaves. Moves out. I am no longer part of their tug-of-war.

Mom says she's sorry. Says it's not my fault. I know, I guess. They always fought.

3

Mom is great at "mom" stuff. But sometimes she drives me nuts. She worries. And now that Dad's gone, she doesn't stop. Jeez. He's only been gone a few days.

"MOM STUFF"

CHANGE   HANG   RECYCLE

"What's wrong, Zeke?"

"You look down."

"School okay?"

"You okay?"

"Talk to me. You can tell me."

"What's wrong?"

I reply with my usual.

"Nothing, Mom."

"I'm fine."

"Fine, Mom."

"Fine, okay?"

"I. Am. Fine."

"Nothing."

"I hate that word," she says.

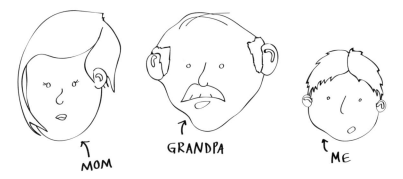

MOM

GRANDPA

ME

Home now is Mom, Grandpa, and me. It feels like a new life. One I don't want. But school is the same. Always. Boring.

Then this new kid shows up. Out of

nowhere. He seems normal. But he isn't. He is my first "visitor."

I have a gift. That's what Grandpa calls it. But it doesn't feel like one. Not even close.

2
THE NEW KID

A new kid? Where Tim Shay used to sit. The bell rings. Morning work at our desks. Same every morning. It's a word search. State capitals.

RIIIIING!

Tim got moved. Far from Max Fisk. Max is a bully. Pretty sure he's fourteen. Way big for sixth grade. Max "likes" Tim. For swirlies, atomic wedgies, mean stuff. Tim is in Mrs. Somer's class now.

← THE WORST
FOR WEDGIES

A-U-S-T-I-N. I can't focus. *B-O-I-S-E.* This new kid has no books. No paper. Nothing. And he just sits there. *D-O-V-E-R.*

I keep at the word search. *S-A-L-E-M.* No use. I can't. So I side stare. Sneak a peek. He's looking around. I *have* to say something.

"Hey, morning work's up there." I point to the front table. "It's a word search," I say. "Know your capitals? We're doing states."

New kids are jumpy. Not this one. He keeps smiling. Dorky smile.

Our teacher says nothing. Hmm. That's weird. She gets right into the lesson.

"Okay, class, who can name the Midwest states?"

The new kid keeps smiling. What a first day! I feel bad. I want to help him. But Mrs. Barns ignores him. Doesn't even do her "new kid" thing. Awkward.

After recess he's gone. His chair is empty.

It's night. My room is black. My eyes close. I open them. Close them. Open them. Close them. Try to focus in the dark. See how long it takes.

I can make out my stuff. Then I turn cold. I shut my eyes. Squeeze them tight. No way. It can't be.

There he is. The new kid. Sitting in my beanbag chair. That dorky smile. Smirk? I dive for the door. Scream down the stairs.

"He's in my room! The new kid! He's up there! Mom!"

Mom gets a heavy pan. She goes to my room. I follow.

3
THE GIFT

She's at my door. I'm impressed. She's super quiet. Not a peep. She stabs a finger at the stairs. She wants me to go. I don't. I shake my head.

I hear two voices. My mind races. One is old. I stare at Mom. I'm scared now. I don't think she hears what I hear. She looks … calm.

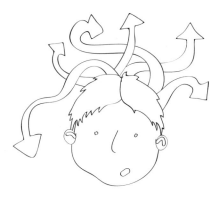

Then it hits me. What are we doing? Our weapon is a frying pan? She rushes in before I can yell. She's waving the pan.

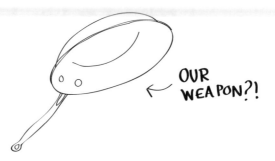

OUR WEAPON?!

"Get out of our house!" she screams. "I called the police." A lie.

"Emma, what are you doing?" Grandpa says. He's on my bed. All casual. He's alone.

"What's going on, Dad?" The pan goes down.

"I heard Zeke yelling. I came down."

"But the new kid. A boy. He was there!" I point at my beanbag chair. I start looking around.

"A boy?" they say at the same time.

"I saw this boy," I say. "The new kid in my class. I was in bed. He was there. Honest!"

They both look at me like I am losing it.

"I bet you were dreaming," Mom says. She gives Grandpa a look. He brushes it off. What's going on between them?

"Zeke, you saw a boy?" Grandpa asks.

"Yeah, from my class," I say. "New kid. Sat next to me."

"And he was in your room just now?"

"Well … um, yeah." Maybe I'm nuts.

AM I NUTS?

Maybe Dad's leaving is harder on me than I thought.

"Zeke, I think you dreamed it," Mom says. "I'm glad I didn't hit you, Dad." She smiles.

"Me too, Emma," Grandpa says. "You're tough. That's my girl."

"Zeke, wanna come down?" Mom asks.

"Stay, Zeke," Grandpa says. "Hang for a bit. Then you can go back to bed. Okay?"

Mom looks at the clock. She nods. Shares another look with Grandpa. What's going on? Then she leaves.

We go to Grandpa's room. It's in the attic. It's cool. Like his own apartment.

GRANDPA'S ATTIC OFFICE

"Have a seat," he says. I like his chairs. Leather. Smooth, dark, kind of shiny. I sink into one. Grandpa sits too. Old maps are behind him on the wall. "It's time you know."

"Know what?" I ask. Something is up.

"You have a gift. We both do. I was about your age."

↖ A GIFT?

"Huh? What, Grandpa?" I say.

"I talked to the boy. His name is Andrew." He smiles. "Nice kid. He's a soccer player. Like you."

"Wait, what?"

15

"Zeke, he told me he needs you," Grandpa says. "They need us."

"Us?" I say. "They?" I still don't get it.

"The living. They need the living. Those with the gift. You have that gift, Zeke. Andrew had cancer. He died not too long ago." Grandpa's face looked sad. "Poor boy. Too young."

Then it hit me. He wasn't joking. My hands shake. So do my legs.

The new kid is dead. He's a ghost!

4
TRENTON, NEW JERSEY

My heart pounds. I take a peek. He isn't there. I breathe. Then go in.

Morning work. Done. No ghost. Feeling better.

Next is social studies.

"Who can tell me the capital of New Jersey?" Mrs. Barns asks.

No hands go up. *New Jersey. New Jersey.*
I know it.

A voice says, "Trenton."

That's it! I was so close, I think.

"Anyone?" Mrs. Barns asks.

"Trenton," the voice says again.

"Need a clue?" she adds. "Starts with *T*."

TRENTON

"Come on, Zeke. Giving you the answer,"
says the voice.

I turn. There he is. The dorky smile.

I yell, "Trenton!"

All heads turn. Andrew. The ghost.
Laughs.

"Wow, dude. Really know your capitals."
He looks smug.

"You got it, Zeke. Somebody's awake."
Mrs. Barns sighs.

Andrew won't shut up. Not a word
yesterday. Today, big mouth.

"Oh, Zeke, that's wrong," he says in math.
"I was great in math. Just sayin'."

When we're reading *A Year Down Yonder*,
he says, "Bo-ring." I give him that one. I'm
not into it.

During science, he won't shut up. Sings

Drake songs. Loud. Off key. I lose it. "Shut up!" I yell. All heads turn. Again.

Mrs. Barns looks shocked.

Ellie Jackson, who sits next to me, purses her lips.

Max says, "No, you shut up, Zeke."

"Max, get to work," Mrs. Barns snaps.

I put my head down. Nobody looks at me.

"What? Don't like Drake?" Andrew says, smiling. He is standing now. In front of me.

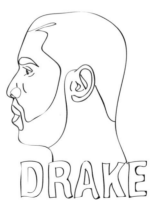

DRAKE

"Used to," I say into my desk.

"Shhh," says Ellie. I ignore her.

"Hey, you're alive. I'm a ghost," Andrew says. "Know what? Ghosts are people too." Then he laughs.

I look at him. He's just a kid like me. Spiky brown hair. Nice shirt. Shorts. Cool sneakers. He looks familiar. But I can't place him.

SPIKY HAIR

NICE SHIRT

COOL SNEAKERS

"We'll talk soon. Gotta see my ... well, gotta go." He looks sad.

I blink. And he's gone.

It's just before bed. Grandpa comes down.

"How you doing?" he asks. "Zeke, I know how you feel. I found out a long time ago," he says. "I know the gift is hard. At first."

"Grandpa," I say. "I don't ... I don't want this." Then I cry.

He hugs me.

I DON'T CRY A LOT

"I know. I didn't either," he says. "I'll help.

Okay? It's hard now. One day …" He sighs. "You'll see the gift for what it is. I swear."

He leaves. How can I help Andrew? I'm just a kid.

5
THE
LOCKER ROOM

The next day I am ghost free. No Andrew.
Only gym and science left. Then home.

Gym is boring. Not big on Ping-Pong.

In the locker room, two things go down.
Max has found another kid to swirly.

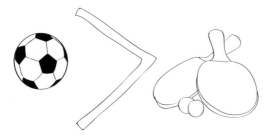

"Stop! Max, no!" Luke Kline begs.

"You're up, Kline. Swirly time!" Max has him off the floor. Luke's feet dangle. "Come on. Take it like a man." The toilet is steps away.

There's a crowd. "Swir-ly! Swir-ly! Swir-ly! Swir-ly!" they chant.

Luke is on his knees now. He's crying. Max pushes his head down. I cut into the crowd. I'm shoving. I grab Max. Push him out of the way. Luke gets up. There's silence.

"Ohh," someone says.

Max turns red. He stares at me. Luke takes off.

"You're dead, Zeke Easton! You're mine!" he spits.

I stand my ground. Max stops. Stares ahead.

Mr. Chase yells, "Who got a swirly?"

My class splits to their lockers.

"Nobody! Nobody!" Max's hands go up. He's on thin ice. He knows it.

Mr. Chase glares at me. Right at me. "Zeke, what's going on?"

I glared at Max. "Nothing. Just paper hoops ... in the trash can."

PAPER HOOPS →

"That's a waste," Mr. Chase says. He knows I'm lying. "Get dressed, both of you!" He turns. Glares at Max. Then he leaves.

Max sneers. Bumps my shoulder hard. Goes to his locker.

MAX'S LOCKER

I can hear kids talking. Nobody can believe it. Luke is quiet. His head is low. I give him a fist bump.

Max is a jerk. He makes kids feel bad. I hate him. I couldn't watch him do it again. It's not right. But now I'm on his list. I know it. He knows it.

SWIRLY LIST

~~CAM~~
~~BRIAN~~
~~LUKE~~
ZEKE

Science is my last class. We watch a video. I shut my eyes. My head hurts. Nothing is right.

"Wow, that dude is a jerk. Max, right?" It's Andrew.

I don't look at him.

"Saw you help Luke," he says. "Brave. Or dumb. Not sure."

29

"Dude, you're not helping," I say. "He's going to beat the crap out of me."

"Uh-huh," Andrew says. "You're toast."

I'M TOAST

"Gee, thanks." I put my head down.

"I have a plan," Andrew says.

"Just go away," I whisper. "I could have used you back there. What good are you?"

This gift sucks.

"No, really," he says. "Listen."

I listen. I perk up. I didn't know ghosts could do that. Isn't it against the rules or something? I can't wait for science to end.

6
REVENGE

I know Max is waiting. But I have a secret weapon. I have Andrew. The ghost.

The bell rings. The class empties fast. I know what's coming. Max is waiting. The entire school is waiting. I look for Andrew. Gone again. I'm on my own. I gulp.

GULP!

I get my stuff. Head outside.

It's sunny. I can smell fresh-cut grass. This makes me sad. It's time for soccer practice. Dad. But I quit the team. I didn't want to …

I see the crowd. Max is pounding one meaty hand with his other. He's a moose.

"Thought you wouldn't show," he says. He has his fists up.

"You thought wrong. What you did today sucked. You suck," I say.

He takes a swipe at me. I dance away. My heart pounds. At least I can move fast. He lunges again. But something's wrong. What's going on?

Then I know. I see Andrew. He's wrapped himself around Max's legs. Like a pretzel.

"Hey, let me go," Max whines. I can hear giggles from the crowd. "You are in serious trouble," Max yells.

I stand my ground. Max isn't going anywhere. Andrew's got him. I had no idea ghosts were so strong.

"Wedgie!" someone yells.

"It's payback," another kid screams.

Max is getting scared. Andrew is not letting go. Max can't move. And he can't see Andrew. Only I can see him. Because of the gift.

"Wedg-ie! Wedg-ie! Wedg-ie!"

Max is crying now.

"Had enough? How does it feel?" I take my finger and poke Max hard in the chest.

"I ... I can't ... move," he stutters.

Luke is there. He gives Max a tight grin. "Need a tissue, big guy?" he asks. Then he backs away.

NOW WHO'S CRYING?

"Nobody's getting a wedgie," I say. "The bullying stops now. Right, Max?" I look at Andrew. Give him a thumbs-up. Maybe this gift isn't so bad.

"Right," Max says.

"Swear it."

"I swear," he says. Andrew releases his legs. He stands beside me. Puts his arm over my shoulder.

Max takes off. Runs like the wind. His pants are wet. Did he pee?

"Thank you," says Luke.

"How did you do that," asks Tim.

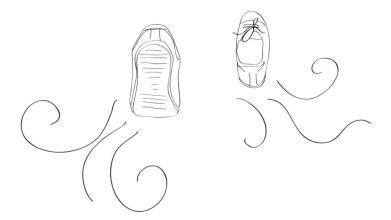

I sigh. Shrug. It's getting late. The crowd

splits up. I start walking home. I look at
Andrew.

"Dude, that was awesome," I say finally.
Andrew grins.

"Play soccer?" I ask him.

"You're on!"

7
A KID LIKE ME

I line the shot. Kick. It feels good. Makes me think of Dad. I miss him. Wonder how he is. Why he hasn't called.

And I miss playing.

Another shot. Sail it.

Then I hear, "You toed it."

"Didn't toe it," I say.

I get the ball. Kick it to him. A clean trap.

It's under his foot. He says, "Ha-ha. Didn't go through me. You thought it would, huh?"

"Okay, yeah," I say.

"I'm solid. For now." He sinks it. Goal!

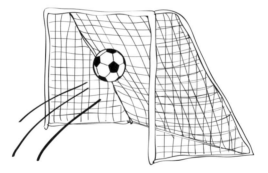

"Not bad," I say.

Wicked shot, I think.

I kick it back.

"For a ghost," I add.

"For a ghost," he agrees.

"Think Max will stop? You know … being such a tool," he asks.

"You scared him, dude," I say. "Felt a little bad."

"Zeke, he had it coming." Andrew rolls his eyes.

"I guess," I say.

"Look, kids like Luke get their lives back. Don't you think?"

"I hope so," I say. Then I snort. "He wet his pants. You really got him. He thought he couldn't move. Everyone laughed. I think he's done being a pig." Then I sigh. "Grandpa told me you got sick."

He takes a long look at me.

"Yeah, I looked like a cue ball. Even lost my eyelashes."

"So where did you live?" I ask.

"Not far from here."

"No way, really?" I look at him again. Maybe I knew him. I shake it off. Nah. "Brothers? Sisters?"

He kicks the ball back. "A sister. She's fifteen."

"Sports? Duh. Oh yeah. Soccer."

"Won state cup," he says. "Twice."

I can tell. Totally. I knew everyone on that state team, didn't I? Dad would know him. Oh. I stop thinking about Dad. *Get out of my head.*

"I play too," I say.

"I know," he says. "I know lots about you. Tell you what." He smiles. "Three shots. Stop a shot? Ask anything you want," he says. "Let any by? No questions."

Now we're talkin'. "Deal," I say.

Then he stares me down. Makes me nervous.

"Ready?"

"Born."

Then he fires. Man, it is wicked!

It stings my hands. Then hits Mom's car.

"Wow. I'm rusty. You know, dead and all."

"Right," I say. "That all you got? Hmm. What should I ask?"

Truth is, my hands kill. His kick? Like an explosion.

"Okay, can you eat?" I ask.

"Don't need to. But I miss pizza," he says.

ANDREW'S FAVORITE

GROSS!
(NOT SUPPOSED TO BE THERE)

He lines up another shot. Kicks. I block it. Burn my hands. Fall down. Get dirt in my mouth.

I get up. Spit out the dirt. Bounce it back to him.

"Not bad," I say.

"You too," he says. "Well?"

"Okay. What did you do for fun?" I ask. *Duh. That was dumb. Not getting a third chance. I know it.*

"Okay, then. Loved to fish. My grandpa took me a lot." He gives me a look. "Um, rule change," he says. "You can ask the last one before I kick."

O Oooo Ooo...
BARRACUDA!

"Okay," I say. *I better make it good. This is my last chance. Why is he here? Why me?*

45

"Come on. Even ghosts don't have all day."

"Why do you need me?"

He smiles.

"Okay, Zeke," he says.

Then he shoots. A blur. Don't stand a chance.

I turn. The ball's in the net. Then I look back. But he's gone. There's just grass. He was just a kid like me. Making wicked shots. Now he's dead.

He doesn't come back that day.

8
GRANDPA'S GROUP

Two days go by. No Andrew. I want him to see. Max isn't Max. He is decent. To me. To Luke. To all of us. Kids snicker. But we all steer clear. It's cool. And weird. The school bully is ... tamed. Guess it worked. Hope it will last.

GOOD BOY, MAX!

I'm reading in my room after school. Someone knocks. It's Grandpa.

"Zeke," he says. "Come up." He turns his head. Looks up. "But be quiet."

So I tiptoe upstairs. He's just ahead. His door is closed.

"Zeke," he says. "I have people in there. My group. We meet every month."

Okay, a group. Huh? Who? I think.

"Zeke, I need to know," he says.

"Know what?" I ask.

"That you'll be okay," he says. "With this. My group. Well, they—"

"They're dead, Grandpa," I say. Nod my head.

"Yes. They're dead. You got it," he says. "Most, long dead."

He looks at me. Pats my shoulder. Says, "Yeah, you'll be okay. Strong kid. I've been keeping an eye. You and Andrew. Doing better than I did at first."

"What do I do here?" I ask.

"Just go in. Sit. Listen. They know you're coming. Okay?"

"Yeah, I think. Yeah, I'm good," I say.

He opens the door.

I see three sets of legs. I keep my head low. My heart races. I sit. Then I look up.

49

My jaw drops. I stare. Holy cow! I know these people. Well, I don't *know-know* them. I've read about them.

There are two men. George Washington. I freak out a little. Albert Einstein is next. Freakin' $E = mc^2$. There's a lady too. I know her. But her name … What *is* her name?

"Zeke," Grandpa says. "I'd like for you to meet George Washington, Albert Einstein, and Mrs. Rosa Parks. My monthly group."

That's it! Rosa Parks. Read about her. About the bus boycott. Civil rights.

Then they talk. I listen.

"You had to work for things," Washington says. "For your food. Clothes. Shelter."

Einstein says, "Yes, today's tech has lots of negatives. But look at all the good."

"Oh, I agree with Al," Rosa Parks says. "The mobile phones … I wish I had one back in the day. We could have organized so much faster."

"Don't tell me, George, that you liked all that physical work. The lack of medicine. So many of your men died at Valley Forge," Einstein says.

George Washington snorts, then folds his arms. Didn't answer.

"Oh, George. You know he's right. Such a stubborn old general," says Mrs. Parks.

And this goes on.

It doesn't seem real.

They talk about the world. Crime. Poverty. Medicine. Space. Bad stuff. Good stuff. I'm dying to ask questions. But Grandpa didn't say I could talk. So I sit. Listen. Absorb. I have a gift. And it's looking pretty cool to me.

Later, I go to bed. I can't sleep. Thinking. Thinking. Thinking.

I was with them. I heard them. They're dead. But they're here. In my freakin' house.

9
ANDREW'S ANSWER

Pop. Andrew's back. It's a Saturday. He's chilling in my beanbag chair.

HE'S BACK

"Getting better, Zeke," he says. "You don't jump anymore. It's been a few days. I had stuff to do," he says. "Ready now?"

"For what?"

"Your answer," he says. "You know. Your last question."

"Oh," I say. "You never did answer."

He smiles. "Nope. Wanna know or not?"

I nod. "Why me?" Stare at him.

"Come here." He puts his arm out. I grab it. Drag him to his feet. He's not light. Weird.

Then there's darkness. I'm not standing. I'm … floating. I hear Andrew. "They can't see us," he says.

WHOA!

I think, *What?* Then we're in a park. It's familiar. Maybe I've played here. There's a soccer team. Kids my age. They're taking practice shots. The goalie is good. I squint. The goalie is … a girl. I *know* her.

I look at him. Andrew. The ghost. Suck in my breath. County All-Stars. We were on the All-Stars team. Her. Me. Andrew.

I choke up. "Andrew," I gasp. "You won MVP. It was just last year."

"Yeah," he says. "Lots can happen in a year. That's Leah. Remember?"

I laugh. Can't help myself. Leah is tough.

She bailed us out. We won because of her. Well, her and Andrew. I helped. But nothing like those two.

"So many practices here," Andrew says.

It's a nice park. Lots of soccer fields. Trees. Places to sit. It's on the other side of the county. My team didn't play here much.

Andrew looks at a bench. A woman sits there. She's watching the team practice.

"My house isn't far," he says. "That is my mom."

I blink. Finally realize we are far from

home. "How did we get here so fast?"

"A ghost thing," he says. "Mom comes here a lot. She's sad. I can't leave her. Not like this. That's why I need you. You need to tell her. Tell her I'm all right," he says. His voice cracks.

He looks away. I see him rub his eyes. "My dad and sister … They're gonna be okay. But her? I'll be right here," he says.

"I thought nobody can see me," I say.

"I can fix that," Andrew says. "Can you help? Please?"

"Yeah. We were a team. A winning team. But even if we just met, I'd help," I say.

"That's why I chose you," he says. "I knew you would."

We walk over.

"My last name is—"

"West," I say. "You're Andrew West. Hard

59

to forget, dude. You were a great player. You were all my dad could talk about. For weeks." I sigh.

Poof. He's gone. Then I see him standing behind his mom.

I come forward. Clear my throat. Take a breath. She looks up.

I say, "Mrs. West?" My voice sounds high. Squeaky.

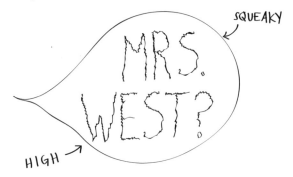

She looks at me. "Yes? Do I know you?"

"No. You don't. But your son does," I say. "Did."

"You knew my son?"

"We were on All-Stars," I say. This is awkward. "But …" I'm not sure what to say next.

"Tell her I'm here," Andrew says. "Tell her … say this is where she'd watch me practice."

I gulp. "He wants me to tell you. You'd watch his practices here."

"What? What's your name?"

"He's behind you," I say. "He's been visiting me. You see. I have this gift." I sound so lame. Crazy. This poor lady.

She gets up. Starts to walk away.

Andrew tells me what to say next.

"Please. Listen. He's telling me. He was little. His first practice. He was scared. He wanted to quit. You told him something. You said it here." Then I tell her what Andrew tells me. Word for word.

She stops. Turns. Her eyes are big.

"Yes," she gasps. "I told him, 'You can quit. But then you'll never know. You'll never know if you're any good. Or how good you could've been.' "

She comes back. Sits down again. There are tears. A lot of them. Andrew sits next to her.

RAINING
TEARS

"Is he really here?"

"Yes, ma'am," I say. "He just sat down next to you."

"I miss him so much," she says.

"He's really worried," I say. "He wants you to be happy." I groan. "Dude," I say. "I am not doing that." I make a face at Andrew.

Then I look at his mom. I start to sing. I'm terrible. "You are my sunshine. My only sunshine—"

Mrs. West starts laughing. And crying. She tells me to stop. Practically begs me.

Thank God.

"Is he okay?" she asks.

"He's great," I say. "He says he will always be with you."

Andrew puts his arm over her shoulder. Squeezes her. Hard.

She inhales. "I can feel him! I can smell him too. Oh!"

They stay that way for a while. I step back. Watch Leah defend the goal. She's cuter than I remember.

Andrew finally let's go. Says good-bye to his mom. She must hear him. She says good-bye too.

Then I am in my room. Alone.

10
GOOD-BYE

It's Sunday. I need to talk to Mom.

"Mom," I say. "Dad called. Yesterday."

She looks mad.

"And how is your dad?" she snips.

"Good," I say.

She smirks.

MOM
SMIRK

"I want to play again," I tell her. "Soccer."

"But you hate playing," she says.

"Mom, you hate me playing. Because you hate Dad."

She looks at me. She looks at the floor.

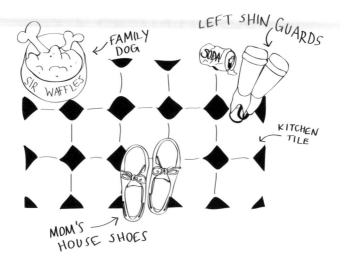

"I like playing. Dad and I talked," I say. "He knows he was too tough. He misses me," I add. "I miss him. I miss my friends. I told him I'd come back. I'm just a kid on his team. He promises. He's in it for fun. He says he'll try."

I don't tell her I want to make All-Stars.

I know Leah will make it. And I want to see her again. If I don't see Andrew ... Leah knew him. And she's, well, pretty ...

"I'm sorry," she says. "I haven't listened. I was jealous." She hugs me. "I'll try to not be a jerk."

"You're not a jerk, Mom," I say.

Grandpa walks in. "Group hug," he says.

He hugs us both. Tight. My mom laughs.

"Mind if I have Zeke for a bit?" he asks Mom.

"Nope. Take him."

"Come on up, Zeke," he says.

I follow him. We go to his room. We sit down in the soft leather chairs.

SO COMFY!

"You didn't tell Mom yet," I say. "She doesn't know."

"She's not ready. Your mom is going through some stuff."

Yeah. I'll say. I fold my arms. "Does she have the gift?"

"She does. But she hasn't been open for a long time," Grandpa says. Then he sighs. "She needs to find herself again. Forgive your dad. It will come back." He rubs his eyes. "I'm very proud of you."

"For what?" I ask.

"Andrew." He pats my back. "Very proud."

I nod. Blink. I haven't seen Andrew today. Is he gone? Am I done? I don't know.

"I'm going to be here. To help. Answer your questions," he says.

"Do you know," I ask. Pause. Breathe.

"Will I know when the next visit ..." My voice trails off.

"It's always a surprise. A good surprise," Grandpa says.

"Okay," I say.

He looks at me. Smiles. "Chess?" he asks.

"Sure," I say.

We're working in pairs. It's Monday. I watch Max. He's helping Luke.

"He's a changed kid." It's Andrew. He looks different. Lighter. He's sitting in an empty desk.

I am happy to see him. Relieved.

"Thanks, Max," I hear Luke say.

Max smiles.

"Yup," I say. "Changed kid."

"That's not in the lesson," Ellie says. "We're on page eighty."

Then Andrew says, "Thank you, Zeke. My family's gonna be okay. Thanks to you."

"Why didn't you tell me?" I whisper. "About All-Stars."

"What?" Ellie is fed up. "Zeke."

I shush her. "Just a sec. I need to say something to my friend." She blinks. Looks at her book.

"You needed to see it," Andrew says. "That's why I picked you. We're a lot the same. I needed someone who kinda knew me. Before." He stands up. "And Leah needs you."

He grins. I smile back.

"Good-bye, my friend," he says. He stands up. Gives me a long look. I blink and he's gone. No walking into the light. Just gone.

I feel good. Happy. Sad.

Ellie pokes me. "Page eighty, I know. Jeez." I get back to the book.

Soccer practice is tonight. I smile. It is going to be okay.